TOP TRADE
C REE

CONSTRUCTION MANAGER

A Crabtree Branches Book

B. Keith Davidson

T0014772

CRABTREE
Publishing Company
www.crabtreebooks.com

School-to-Home Support for Caregivers and Teachers

This high-interest book is designed to motivate striving students with engaging topics while building fluency, vocabulary, and an interest in reading. Here are a few questions and activities to help the reader build upon his or her comprehension skills.

Before Reading:

- *What do I think this book is about?*
- *What do I know about this topic?*
- *What do I want to learn about this topic?*
- *Why am I reading this book?*

During Reading:

- *I wonder why...*
- *I'm curious to know...*
- *How is this like something I already know?*
- *What have I learned so far?*

After Reading:

- *What was the author trying to teach me?*
- *What are some details?*
- *How did the photographs and captions help me understand more?*
- *Read the book again and look for the vocabulary words.*
- *What questions do I still have?*

Extension Activities:

- *What was your favorite part of the book? Write a paragraph on it.*
- *Draw a picture of your favorite thing you learned from the book.*

IN A COMMUNITY

In a community, people live and work together to make their neighborhood a better place.

From the doctors who heal the sick, to the waiters who serve us food, everyone has a role to play to contribute to the growth of the community.

Construction managers oversee the building of houses, shopping centers, and office buildings.

They manage **budgets**, order supplies, and deal with the everyday business of running the jobsites.

Who is the construction manager? Look for the person in the white hard hat.

WHAT DO I NEED?

Can you multitask? Can you handle the pressure of dealing with plumbers, carpenters, and electricians all at the same time? If so, you could be a construction manager.

You need to have a high school diploma and often a degree in architecture, engineering, or construction. But these are not the only paths you can take. Professional **certifications** are also important, and some states require construction managers to be licensed.

Are construction managers the same as architects? No. Architects design buildings. Construction managers supervise the construction of buildings.

SPECIAL SKILLS

Construction managers need specialized skills to do their job. They have to be able to read **blueprints** and understand how the building is supposed to come together.

They must have a knowledge of plumbing, electrical, carpentry, and other **trades** involved in the project.

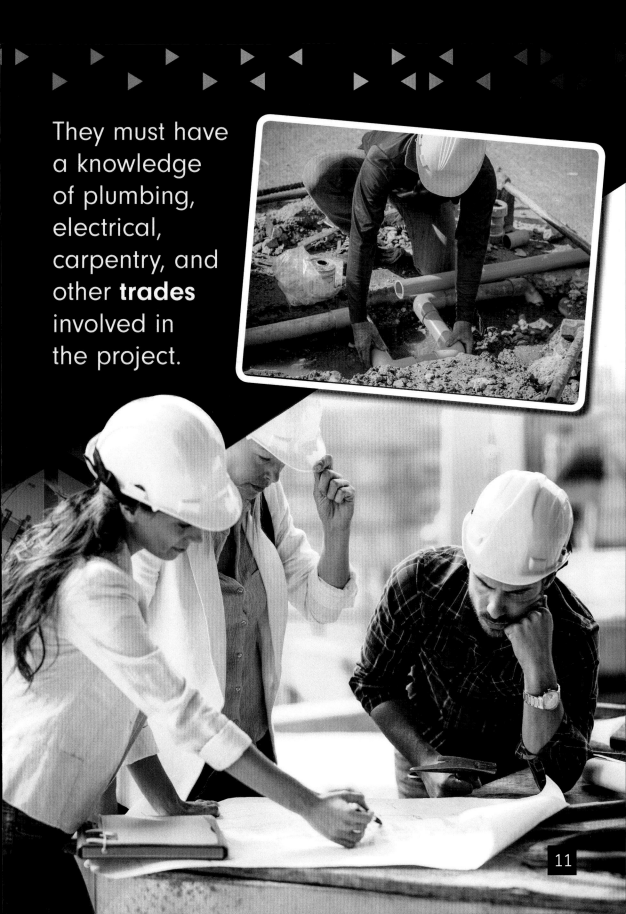

A construction manager must be able to **estimate** the costs of the materials and the workers needed to get the project completed. They need to keep each job within a budget.

Time is another factor. A construction manager has to figure out a **schedule** for each job.

Many construction managers use computer programs to provide cost estimates and to figure out schedules for their projects.

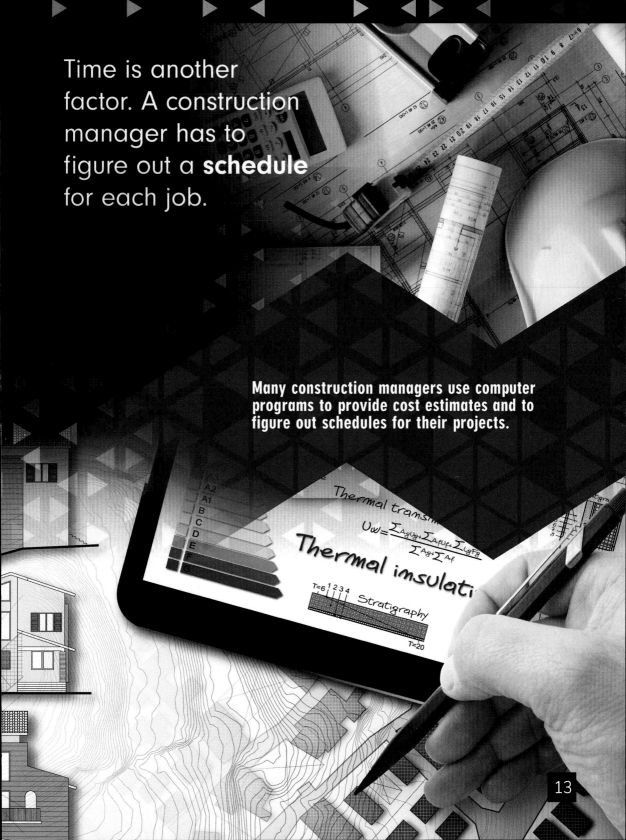

A construction manager must be organized. The **tradespeople** are only responsible for their part of the project.

The construction manager has to organize the project and make sure that the tradespeople work on the project in an order that is the most **efficient**.

WORKING CONDITIONS

Construction managers are often **self-employed**, but some may belong to a large construction firm or even a small company.

They may have a permanent office, but in many cases their office is a **mobile** one that moves from jobsite to jobsite.

A big part of the construction manager's job is meeting with clients and going over their **vision** for the project.

These meetings will involve going over schedules, budgets, and other concerns that the clients may have about the project.

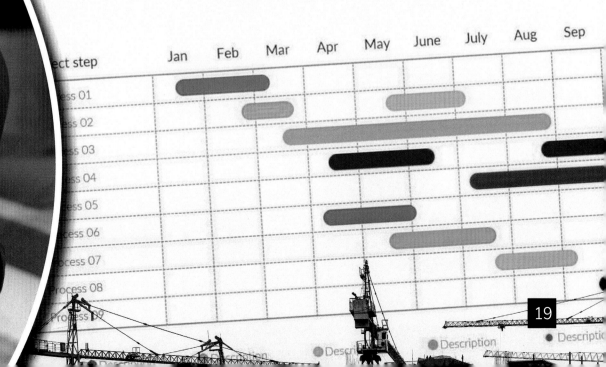

Project Schedule

ect step	Jan	Feb	Mar	Apr	May	June	July	Aug	Sep
ess 01									
ess 02									
ess 03									
ess 04									
ess 05									
ess 06									
cess 07									
ocess 08									
Process 09									

The construction manager will also start to purchase the **materials** for the job and plan out the work schedule for the project.

Construction managers need to have a great deal of knowledge when it comes to workplace safety. They need to make sure that the workers will be safe.

SITE SAFETY

	Hard hat must be worn	⚠ ⚠	**Warning** Construction site **Keep out**
	Protective footwear must be worn	⚠	**Danger** Demolition work in progress
	High visibility jackets must be worn	🚫	No admittance for unauthorised personnel
	Ear protectors must be worn	✓	Site safety starts here

Environmental safety
is also a concern.

Choosing the materials and organizing how waste is disposed allows the manager to decide how environmentally friendly the job will be.

NOT ALWAYS EASY

Being a construction manager isn't an easy job. Some projects may run smoothly, but there are often problems along the way.

Sometimes the materials will be delivered late, or the electricians will still be working when the drywall is scheduled to be put up. Problems arise on jobsites and it is the manager's job to deal with each one.

MAKING A LIVING

Being a construction manager is a fast-paced and in-demand career that often pays very well.

The salary depends on many different things including location, the type of projects, and the client's budget.

City Works (e.g. roads, bridges)	$90,000 - $102,000
Office Buildings/Malls	$80,000 - $98,000
Specialty Trade (e.g. concrete, electrical)	$77,700 - $93,000
Residential	$75,000 - $89,000

Construction managers are important members of their communities. They create jobs and keep workers safe. They help create the homes, roads, and other buildings that make up our communities.

GLOSSARY

blueprints (BLOO-prints): drawings that show how a building will fit together

budgets (BUHJ-its): plans for spending money

certifications (sur-tuh-fi-KEY-shuhnz): proof of skills in a trade

efficient (uh-FISH-uhnt): works very well and wastes no time or energy

environmental (en-VYR-ruh-MEN-tuhl): relating to the natural world of land, water, and air

estimate (ESS-ti-muht): a rough calculation

materials (muh-TIHR-ee-uhlz): the supplies needed to construct a building

mobile (MOH-buhl): able to move

schedule (SKEJ-ool): timetable

self-employed (SELF-im-ployd): a person who works for themselves

trades (TREYDZ): careers that involve hands-on work and specialty knowledge

tradespeople (TREYDZ-PEE-puhl): those skilled in a trade, such as a carpenter or plumber

vision (VIZH-uhn): something imagined

INDEX

WEBSITES TO VISIT

www.bls.gov/ooh/management/
construction-managers.htm#tab-1

www.goconstruct.org/construction-careers/
what-jobs-are-right-for-me/construction-manager

www.conserve-energy-future.com/
sustainable-construction-materials.php

ABOUT THE AUTHOR

B. Keith Davidson has had careers in agriculture, industrial manufacturing, and the service industry. His career in education led to his current career in writing books.

CRABTREE
Publishing Company

Written by: B. Keith Davidson

Designed by: Jennifer Dydyk

Edited by: Kelli Hicks

Proofreader: Ellen Rodger

Print and production coordinator: Katherine Berti

Photographs: Cover career logo icon © Trueffelpix, diamond pattern used on cover and throughout book © Aleksandr Andrushkiv, cover photo © Kzenon, tools photo at top of cover and on title page © Aleksandar Grozdanovski, Page 4 © wavebreakmedia, Page 5 top photo © fizkes, bottom photo © FamVeld, Page 6 © Stuart Monk, Page 7 top photo © ESB Professional, bottom photo © mdgn, Page 8 © Bannafarsai_Stock, Page 9 top photo © G-Stock Studio, middle photo © Narin Nonthamand, bottom photo © Supavadee butradee, Page 10 top photo © PV productions, bottom photo © Maksym Dykha, Page 11 top photo © EsanIndyStudios, bottom photo © BalanceFormCreative, Page 12 top photo © Dragon Images, photo across bottom of page 12 and 13 © Francesco Scatena, Page 13 top photo © Zolnierek, Page 14 © Naparat, Page 15 top photo © sirtravelalot, bottom photo © Gorodenkoff, Page 16 © dotshock, Page 17 top photo © A Lot Of People, bottom photo © Svitlana Hulko, Page 18 © A Lot Of People, Page 19 top photo © Francesco Scatena, bottom photo © Mongkolchon Akesin, Page 20 © Pincasso, Page 21 top photo © frantic00, bottom photo © Syda Productions, Page 22 top photo © John Williams RUS, Page 23 © romul 014, Page 24 © MilanMarkovic78, Page 25 top photo © Whyimage, bottom photo © Kent E Roberts, Page 26 © romul 014, Page 27 © 1599686sv, Page 28 © StreetonCamara, Page 29 top photo © NP27, bottom photo © Andy Dean Photography. All images from Shutterstock.com

Library and Archives Canada Cataloguing in Publication

Available at the Library and Archives Canada

Library of Congress Cataloging-in-Publication Data

Available at the Library of Congress

Crabtree Publishing Company

www.crabtreebooks.com   1-800-387-7650

Copyright © 2022 **CRABTREE PUBLISHING COMPANY**

Published in the United States
Crabtree Publishing
347 Fifth Avenue
Suite 1402-145
New York, NY, 10016

Published in Canada
Crabtree Publishing
616 Welland Ave.
St. Catharines, ON
L2M 5V6

Printed in Canada/082022/CPC20220818